Chips
Wisdom, Sacred and Profane

Chips

Wisdom, Sacred and Profane

Peter N Roth, babe-chick

Saint Mechtilde, The Love of the Sacred Heart, ISBN 9781492963714

A Benedictine Monk, IN SINU JESU: When Heart speaks to Heart. The journal of a priest at prayer. © Angelico Press, angelicopress.com, ISBN 9781621382195

Scripture quotations labeled NRSV are from the New Revised Standard Version Catholic Edition copyright © 1993 and 1989 by the Division of Christian Education of the National Council of the Churches of Christ in the U.S.A. Used by permission. All rights reserved.

Unless otherwise noted, the scripture quotations contained herein are from the Jerusalem Bible copyright © 1966 by Darton, Longman & Todd, Ltd. and Doubleday & Company, Inc. Used by permission. All rights reserved.

ISBN-13: 979-8667966487

Dedication

To the Team of the 66th Mens' Cursillo, and to all Cursillistas of the Arlington Cursillo Movement, especially those in their 4th and 5th days.

At that time Jesus said, "I thank you, Father, Lord of heaven and earth, because you have hidden these things from the wise and the intelligent and have revealed them to infants; yes, Father, for such was your gracious will." Matthew 11:25-26 (NRSV).

Foreword

Pete Roth is an old (long term 😊) friend of mine. As you read and reflect on these "chips," you will begin to get to know my friend Pete—his values—his humor—his caring.

Pete calls these quotes "chips" . They are a collection of pithy thoughts from all kinds of different sources. Some are Pete's own wisdom but most are from Scripture, or the saints, or other wise and thoughtful people. I love one of Pete's own "chips"—"why use a needle when you can use a harpoon"...

Knowing Pete, you are always waiting for the "harpoon"—the direct thought—the direct idea—the direct challenge.

I hope that you will find among these "chips" some harpoons for yourself. This book will fail if it does not provoke you and me to deeper thoughts and more authentic lives.

Pete has left a lot of space in this book for your thoughts and your journaling. I also suggest that you use some of the space provided to collect your own "chips". This book will reach its full potential only if it sparks the reader to explore and meditate on their own bits of wisdom and consolation and challenge.

Have fun with this book. Use it as a "jumping off" point for your own thoughts. Find your own chips that "harpoon" you. Pete has shared some of his own "chips" now find your own! You won't be disappointed.

Tuck Grinnell

Introduction

The Ignatian Exercises

In 2000 AD, Joe McCloskey, SJ asked me after one of our spiritual direction sessions "When are you going to do the Annotation 19 Retreat?" How typical of Joe: Invite me to a thing, about which I knew nothing, and use a cryptic name to do it. But we'd been friends long enough for me to trust him, so I began the "long" Ignatian Exercises with Joe as my Director-Companion.

Ignatius was a soldier, so I think his experience of arranging and scheduling things helped him in the development of his spiritual framework. And of course, the Jesuits.

The exercises involved a modicum of discipline that included evening and morning prayer, daily. (When the exercises were over, it seemed natural to continue some of the discipline in normal life.)

The evening prayer is The Examen, which is a summary of the day, and a plan for tomorrow.

The Morning prayer is a conversation about the day ahead. Ignatius was a practitioner of the freedom of the believer, so the morning conversation is up to Jesus and me. That's where I use these chips.

While I have some ability recognizing wisdom as it applies to me, I fail utterly to reckon the dates, times, and sources of these sayings. I present them here in the approximate order in which I recorded them with pen and ink.

My Morning Prayer

Currently, my practice is to read the scriptures at breakfast. Afterwards, I retreat to a private room and read from, and take notes on:

- *An Ignatian Book of Days*, by Jim Manney, ISBN 978-0829441451 with a reading and meditation for every day of the year.

- I read one of the Chips from this book, and stay with it for a few moments. I do that with that Chip for a week before I move on. When I get to the end of the book, I circle back to the beginning. Since there are over 156 Chips, cycling through the collection takes more than 3 years.

- I use a reading from the lives of the saints. As I write this, I'm reading *A Life of Saint Catherine of Siena* by Paul Murray, OP, ISBN 978-1943243570.

- A reading from *In Sinu Jesu* comes next, followed by one of the chapters from John 13-17.

- I usually write a note in my journal about what has struck me, or what has puzzled me.

- And then, silence, just hanging out with a Friend.

Commendation

Note that these are not *potato* chips, so you don't have to read them all at once.

On the other hand, if you take them one a day like a vitamin pill, there's enough for half a year.

There's enough room in here for short notes. My
notes tend to be long, so I use a separate journal,
and put all my notes in it.

May our Lord Jesus richly bless you as you taste
of these Chips. And may you find Chips of your
own in your own Study!

Peter N Roth, babe-chick

July 9, 2020

The Chips

Rejoice always!

1 Thessalonians 5:16

 1 Thessalonians 5:16

This is the way you ought to talk,
neighbor to neighbor, brother to
brother: "What answer has YHWH
given?" or "What has YHWH said?"

Jeremiah 23:35

Unload all your worries on him, for he
is looking after you.

1 Peter 5:7

Direct, O Lord, I beseech Thee, all my actions by your divine inspirations. Carry them out by your gracious assistance, that every prayer and work of mine might always begin from you, and by you be happily ended.

Saint Ignatius Loyola

Soul of Christ, sanctify us.
Body of Christ, save us.
Blood of Christ, inebriate us.
Water from the side of Christ, wash us.
Passion of Christ, strengthen us.
Sacred Heart of Jesus, have mercy on
us.
Within your wounds, hide us.
Permit us not to be separated from
Thee.
From the wicked foe, defend us.
At the hours of our deaths, call us,
And bid us come to Thee,
That with Thy saints we might praise
Thee
Forever and ever.

The Anima Christi, expanded

Are you people in Galatia *mad*!? Has someone put a spell on you in spite of the plain explanation you've had of the crucifixion of Jesus Christ? Let me ask you one question: was it because you practiced the Law that you received the Spirit, or because you believed what was preached to you? Are you foolish enough to end in outward observances what you began in the Spirit? Have all the favors you've received been *wasted*!? And if this were so, they were most certainly wasted. Does God give you the Spirit so freely and work miracles among you because you practice the Law, or because you believe what was preached to you?

Saint Paul, Galatians 3:1-5

Take, O Lord, and receive my entire
liberty, my memory, my
understanding, and my whole will. All
that I am, and all that I possess You
have given to me. I surrender it all to
Your love and Your grace; with these I
will be rich enough, and will desire
nothing more.

Suscipe

Every cross, great or small, even small
annoyances, are the voice of the
Beloved. He is asking for a declaration
of love from us to last whilst the
suffering lasts.

Charles de Foucauld

When the cross is offered for another,
it becomes redemptive.

Joe McCloskey, SJ

Although we speak of "making friends", friends cannot be made. Friends are gifts from God.

Henri Nouwen

In the beginning was the Word,
and the Word was with God,
and the Word was God.
He was with God in the beginning.
Through him all things came to be,
not one thing had its being but through
him.
All that came to be had life in him,
and that life was the light of Men,
a light that shines in the dark,
a light that darkness could not
overpower.

John 1:1-5

A man came, sent by God.
His name was John.
He came as a witness,
as a witness to speak for the light,
so that everyone might believe
through him.
He was not the light, only a witness to
speak for the light.

John 1:6-8

The Word was the true light that
enlightens all Men;
and he was coming into the world.
He was in the world, that had its being
through him, and the world did not
know him. He came to his own domain,
and his own people did not accept him.
But to all who did accept him,
to them he gave power to become
children of God,
to all who believe in the name of him
who was born not out of human stock,
or urge of the flesh,
or will of man,
but of God himself.
The Word was made flesh,
he pitched his tent among us,
and we saw his glory, the glory that is
his as the only Son of the Father,
full of grace and truth.

John 1:9-14

John appears as his witness. He
proclaims:
"This is the one of whom I said:
he who comes after me
ranks before me
because he existed before me!"

Indeed, from his fullness we have, all
of us, received – yes, grace in return
for grace,
since, though the law was given
through Moses,
grace and truth have come through
Jesus Christ.
No one has ever seen God:
it is the only Son, who is nearest to the
Father's heart, who has made him
known.

John 1:15-18

Change!

Peter N Roth

Stuff Gets Lost, And Found

Sheep:	1%
Drachma:	10%
Sons:	100%

Luke 15

Why use a needle, when a harpoon will
do?

Peter N Roth

Those who fail to admit their
ignorance are destined to remain so.

Peter N Roth

Those who avoid politics are destined
to be ruled by their inferiors.

Plato

I ask the Father to give me an intimate
knowledge of the many gifts received,
so that filled with gratitude for all, I
may in all things love and serve the
divine majesty.

Saint Ignatius Loyola

Prayer for a Cursillo Team
Lord, our efforts are pretty puny.
Please accept all the imperfections we
offer: the inadequate Talks, the missed
guitar notes, the poor song choices,
our failures to love each other, and our
ignorance. It seems that's all we're
going to come up with. Please turn our
lead into Your gold for the benefit of
our Cursillistas. Guide us by Your
Spirit, give us the wisdom to detect
and reject the other spirit, and our
stupidity. Thanks.

Peter N Roth

Fear indeed is nothing other than the abandonment of the supports offered by reason; the less you rely within yourself on these, the more alarming it is not to know the cause of your suffering.

Wisdom 17:11-12

A Rector of a Cursillo knows the
Cursillo is perfect not when there is
nothing left to add, but when there is
nothing left to take away.

Antoine de Saint Exupery (paraphrased)

My son, if you aspire to serve the Lord,
prepare yourself for an ordeal.
Be sincere of heart; be steadfast, and
do not be alarmed when disaster
comes.

Ecclesiasticus 2:1-2

Lord Jesus, two graces I ask of You
before I die:
First, to feel in my soul & in my body,
as far as possible, the sorrow which
Thou, sweet Jesus, didst endure in the
hour of Thy most bitter Passion;
Second, to feel in my heart, as far as
possible, that extraordinary love with
which Thou, O Son of God, wast
inflamed, to the point of willingly
undergoing so great a Passion for us
sinners.

Saint Francis of Assisi

It is right to keep the secret of a king,
yet right to reveal & publish the works
of God. Thank Him worthily, do what is
good, & no evil can befall you.

Tobit 12:7

Happy the husband of a really good wife; the number of his days will be doubled.
A perfect wife is the joy of her husband, he will live out the years of his life in peace.
A good wife is the best of portions, reserved for those who fear the Lord; rich or poor, they will be glad of heart, cheerful of face, whatever the season.

Sirach 26:1-4

I will betroth you to myself forever,
betroth you with integrity & justice,
with tenderness and love; I will
betroth you to myself with
faithfulness, and you will come to
know YHWH.

Hosea 2:21-22

You must live your whole life
according to the Christ you have
received — Jesus the Lord.

Colossians 2:6

In my flesh, I make up what is lacking
in Christ's trials, for the sake of His
Body, which is the church.

Colossians 1:24

But if anyone wants to boast, let him boast of this: of understanding & knowing me. For I am YHWH. I rule with kindness, justice & integrity on earth; yes, these are what please me— it is YHWH who speaks.

Jeremiah 9:23

Live every day as if it were your last.
One day, you'll be right.

Peter N Roth

Follow any way when faith is so
obscure, and darkness obliterates
everything, & the path can no longer
be discerned — for a path cannot be
lost which does not exist.

Jean Pierre de Caussade

What is good has been explained to
you, man–this is what YHWH asks of
you, only this: to act justly, to love
tenderly, and to walk humbly with
God.

Micah 6:8

Am I not to feel sorry for Nineveh, the
great city, in which there are more
than 120,000 people who cannot tell
their right hand from their left, to say
nothing of the animals?

Jonah 4:11

YHWH teach me Your way, how to
walk beside You faithfully. Make me
single-minded in fearing Your name.

Psalm 86:11

YHWH your God is in your midst, a
victorious warrior.
He will exult with joy over you,
He will renew you by his love;
He will dance with shouts of joy for
you as on a day of festival!

Zephaniah 3:17-18a

Glory be to him who can keep you
from falling & bring you safe to his
glorious presence, innocent and happy.
To God, the only God, who saves us
through Jesus Christ our Lord, be the
glory, majesty, authority, & power,
which he had before time began, now
and forever. Amen.

Jude 24,25

The best catechism is to fix our eyes on created things, because through things, God begins to speak to us.

Carlo Caretto

An act of pure faith is death of what we
love most so it may be offered to the
loved one because only love is strong
than death.

Carlo Caretto

And now, Lord, take note of their
threats & help your servants to
proclaim your message with all
boldness, by stretching out your hand
to heal and work miracles & marvels
through the name of your holy servant
Jesus.

Acts 4:29-30

To those who prove victorious I will
give the hidden manna & a white stone
— a stone with a new name written on
it, known only to the one who receives
it.

Revelation 2:17

Anyone who honestly and passionately searches for truth is on the way to Christ.

Edith Stein (St. Teresa Benedicta of the Cross OCD)

This Jesus is the stone rejected by you
the builders; it has become the
cornerstone. There is salvation in no
one else, for there is no other name
under heaven given among mortals by
which we must be saved.

Acts 4:11-12

I will walk in YHWH's presence
in the land of the living.

Psalm 116:18

But you have no right to demand
guarantees where the desires of the
Lord our God are concerned. For God
is not to be coerced as man is, nor is
he, like mere man, to be cajoled.

Judith 8:16

It is not the man who commends
himself that can be accepted, but the
man who is commended by the Lord.

2 Corinthians 10:18

Our help is in the name of YHWH, who
made heaven and earth.

Psalm 124:8

For man, poverty is the thirst for life
without yet possessing life, the search
for the absolute while still living in the
contingent, the hunger for God while
not yet being God, the hope of the
Resurrection while still immersed in
death.

Carlo Caretto

Faith has the dimensions of God,
reason has the dimensions of Man.
Faith opens the secrets of heaven,
reason opens the secrets of earth.
Faith takes you into My presence,
reason into the presence of things.

Carlo Caretto

The heart of the gospel is to make of
ourselves an oasis of love in whatever
desert we might find ourselves.

Robert Ellsberg

Cry out for joy and gladness, you
dwellers in Zion, for great in the midst
of you is the Holy One of Israel.

Isaiah 12:6

God is closer to me than I am to myself;
he is equally close to wood & stone,
but they don't know it.

Meister Eckhart

It is impossible to come into God's
presence.

Peter N Roth

Heaven is for everyone who is willing
to sit down with everyone.

John Shea

Is God less inventive than we are? If
we were designing how things worked,
would we let death be the end of it?

Carlo Caretto

<u>Grace before meals</u>:
Dear Lord,
Thanks for the food before us,
The family and friends beside us,
And Your love around us.

Carol Lahti

You are as sick as your sickest secret,
and you will remain sick as long as it
remains a secret.

Alcoholics Anonymous

Scripture uses the expression "The
Body of Christ" to mean three things:
Jesus, the historical person;
Eucharist, which is also the physical
presence of God among us;
The Body of Believers, which is also
the real presence.

Ron Rolheiser

The church is based on gathering
around the person of Jesus & sharing
his Spirit.

Ron Rolheiser

Who is my neighbor? My neighbor is
the person who is already in my life
while I am plotting how to be in
someone else's life.

Ron Rolheiser

Fear not—you ARE inadequate!

Ron Rolheiser

Four qualities must be tested in a
friend: loyalty, right intention,
discretion, and patience.

Aelred of Rievaulx

The soul does not belong to us, it
belongs to God.

Tilden Edwards

We would be surprised to know what
our souls are saying to God.

Brother Lawrence

We would be surprised to know what
our souls are saying to one another.

Tilden Edwards

The language of God is the experience
that God writes into our lives.

San Juan de Cruz

I am the resurrection and the life. If anyone believes in me, even though they die, they shall live, and anyone who lives and believes in me shall never die. Do you believe this?

John 11:25-26

Everything is on loan.

Peter N Roth

Fear not! The things you are afraid of
may indeed happen to you, but they
are nothing to be afraid of.

John McMurray

Just because you can't understand
something doesn't mean it isn't true.

Saint Thomas Aquinas

Everything matters!
Everything is holy!

All that I see is a distraction from
seeing God.

Joe McCloskey, SJ

In every moment, God is loving us in
thousands of ways. All we need do is
touch one of them to have them all.

Joe McCloskey, SJ

However impressive may be one's
knowledge or experience of God, that
knowledge and that experience will
have no resemblance to God, and
amount to very little.

Saint John of the Cross

It is not for me to be successful or to
measure success, but to do & be with
joy.

Peter N Roth

Why cling to what I cannot keep, when
I can exchange it for that which I
cannot lose?

People *always* hear words of praise.

Peter N Roth

With that Moon Language

Admit something:
Everyone you see, you say to them
"Love me!"
Of course you do not say this out loud.
Otherwise
Someone would call the cops.
Still, though, think about this,
This great pull to connect.
Why not become the one
Who lives with a full moon in each eye
That is always saying
With that sweet moon
Language
What every other eye in this world
Is dying to
Hear.

Hafez

Art is never finished; it's abandoned.

Leonardo Da Vinci

Small steps + Small chunks +
Perseverance = Progress.

Peter N Roth

If you're in a market & someone's
trying to sell you something you don't
understand, you should think that
they're selling you a lemon.

George Akerlof

What am I to do with Jesus, who is
called the Christ?

Pontius Pilate, Matthew 27:22

To be too much bothered by questions we cannot answer is to be irked at not being God. Above all we must not be so bothered by the darkness ringing our circle of light that we cannot enjoy the light.

Frank Sheed

For people of faith, there are no coincidences; only aspects of God's providence not fully understood.

Pope Saint John Paul II

God is not offended by us except at
what we do against our own good.

Thomas Aquinas

Non nissite Domine.

Thomas Aquinas

I am a sinner who has been looked on
by God.

Pope Francis I

There are no interruptions.

Peter N Roth

Reproving a Christian who sins:
By 1.
By 2.
By All.
Bye bye.

Summary of Mt 18: 15-19

God provides for humanity's need, not
for humanity's greed.

Matthew Kelly

Teaching is not bringing people to where I am, but showing them where the road is so they can make their own Journey.

Peter N Roth

Thou are that reality Whose center is
everywhere & Whose circumference is
nowhere.

Hermes Trismegistis

Get naked with God.

Peter N Roth

Get used to the idea that you're a
beginner.

Martin Laird

I'm an old man now & have had a great
many problems. Most of them never
happened.

Mark Twain

Union with God is not something that
is acquired, but realized.

Martin Laird

If your goals are ambitious & crazy enough, even failure will be a pretty good achievement.

Larry Page

Love itself is a kind of knowing.

Saint Gregory the Great

In order to arrive at what you do not
know, you must go by a way which is
the way of ignorance... & what you do
not know is the only thing you know.

T. S. Eliot

Two Rules for becoming a good monk:
     Ask: Who am I?
     Judge no one.

The Desert Fathers

If you can sit and do nothing, you can
do virtually anything.

A short prayer penetrates heaven.

Cloud 37

I invite all Christians, everywhere, at
this very moment, to a renewed
personal encounter with Jesus Christ,
or at least an openness to letting Him
encounter *them*; I ask all of you to do
this unfailingly each day.

Pope Francis I

Any truth that we can grasp &
understand is, in the end, not very
deep.

Ron Rolheiser

Not only has the God we desire already
found us, thus causing our desire, but
God has never NOT found us.

Martin Laird

Do not let your love be a pretense, but
sincerely prefer good to evil. Love each
other as brothers & sisters should, and
have a profound respect for each
other. Outdo each other in mental
esteem.

Saint Paul, Romans 12: 9-10

God invites me to be attentive to the least, the last, and the lost.

Allen Hunt

Remember who you are and where
you are.

Anonymous

Remember where you stand & in
Whose presence.

Anonymous

Virtues come with grace. Then we act
with that virtue & it grows as part of
us.

<u>Anonymous</u>

Anyone who claims to be in the light
but hates his brother is still in the
dark.

I John 2:9

I beg of You, my Lord, to remove
anything which separates me from
You, & You from me.
Remove anything that makes me
unworthy of Your sight, Your control,
Your reprehension; of Your speech &
conversation; of Your benevolence &
love.
Cast from me every evil that stands in
the way of my seeing You, hearing,
tasting, savoring, and touching You;
fearing & being mindful of You;
knowing, trusting, loving, & possessing
You; being conscious of Your presence
&, as far as may be, enjoying You. This
is what I ask for myself & earnestly
desire from You. Amen.

Saint Peter Favre, SJ

The crucifixion is the most important
historical event that ever happened.

The Church

Lord, by Your cross and resurrection,
You have set us free. You are the savior
of the world.

Prayer at Mass

The crucifixion is the touchstone of
Christian authenticity, the unique
feature by which everything else,
including the resurrection, is given its
true significance.

Fleming Rutledge

If Jesus had not been raised from the
dead, we would never have heard of
Him.

Anonymous

And all who touched Him were cured.

Mark 6:56

Do small things. They're the start of an avalanche.

Richard Delillio, OSFD

To confess your sins to God is not to
tell Him anything he doesn't already
know. Until you confess them,
however, they are the abyss between
you. When you confess them, they
become the bridge.

Friedrich Buechner

All are welcome in the Church, but on
Christ's terms, not their own.

Cardinal Francis George

In a higher world it is otherwise, but
here below, to live is to change, & to be
prefect is to have changed often.

An attachment is anything in this world–including your own life–that you are convinced you cannot live without.

Anthony de Mello, SJ

Once the demands of propriety and necessity have been met, the rest of what one owns belongs to the poor.

Pope Leo XIII

Who has two shirts in the closet, one
belongs to them, the other belongs to
one who has no shirt.

Saint Ambrose

There is more to Saint Ignatius than
the Exercises. There's more to
everyone.

Peter N Roth

Thanks for Creation itself.
For my ancestors & those who
struggled to give me life.
For my parents.
For my immediate family, whether
related by blood or not.
For my body, whether I like it or not.
For my wit, whether I have enough or
not.
For my faculties of sense, even if some
seem faulty.
For my special talents, whether or not
I think them useful.
For friends & loved ones, whether alive
or dead.
For my work, whether for money of
not.
for my play, even though it may seem
infrequent.
For my possessions, no matter how
much money they are worth.
For my time to live, no matter how
quickly it seems to pass.

Tim Muldoon

Who finds a spouse finds happiness, a
mark of favor from YHWH.

Proverbs 12:22

O God, You make a way out of no way.

Lezek Kołakowski

Capital punishment means them
without the capital gets the
punishment.

Anonymous

Let us not lose sight of Jesus who leads us in our faith & brings it to perfection. For the sake of the joy which was still in the future, he endured the cross, disregarding the shamefulness of it, & from now on has taken his place at the right of God's throne.

Hebrews 12:2

The punishment for sin is to live a life
of sin.

Peter N Roth

Thomas Aquinas was asked "What must I do to be a saint?" and he said "Will it." Be a Saint, and you'll unleash the power of grace & holiness.

Robert Barron

Ideas! Ideas! What's a few ideas
between friends?

Pope Saint John XXIII

O God, You aren't a being, not even a Supreme Being. You are *ipsum esse subsistens*, that is, subsistent being itself. You are not in the genus of being. You are the *ground* of all being. You are not even in the highest possible genus, the genus of being. You are not an individual. You are not a thing in the world but rather the reason why there's something rather than nothing.

Robert Barron, quoting Thomas Aquinas

In the design of Providence, there are
no mere coincidences.

Pope Saint John Paul II

Christianity is not a formula that makes everything clear, but the radical submission of myself to an incomprehensible Mystery Who has revealed Himself as ineffable love.

Karl Rahner, SJ

There is no need to wear yourself out,
but make a competent & sufficient
effort & leave the rest to Him.

Ignatius Loyola

Part of the struggle of an illness is that
the patient has to fight to become the
subject of his illness instead of simply
remaining the 'object of treatment'.

Pope Saint John Paul II

God is above success and failure.

Anonymous

Work is always a gift of the Lord.

Saint Peter Favre, SJ

By seeking God in good works through
the Spirit, one will more readily find
him afterwards in prayer, than if one
had sought him first in prayer so as to
subsequently find him in good works.

Saint Peter Favre, SJ

Through Your most holy passion and
death I beg of You, Lord, to grant me a
most holy life and a most complete
death to all my vices, and passions, and
self-love and to grant me sight of your
holy faith, hope and charity.

Saint Alphonsus Rodriquez, SJ

May it please the supreme and divine
Goodness to give me abundant grace
ever to know Your most holy will and
perfectly fulfill it.

Saint Ignatius Loyola

In politics, to be deceived is no excuse.

Lezek Kołakowski

I am more attentive in listening to your
prayers than you could ever be in
making them.

Jesus, in In Sinu Jesu

Jesus is out in the street without food, without shelter. What am I doing about it?

Saint Alberto Hurtado, SJ

This is my desire: that your whole life
should reflect, even now, the order and
beauty that characterize my kingdom.
This is also My Mother's desire for you,
& she will help you to attain it.

In Sinu Jesu

People don't stop adoring me because
they've lost their faith; rather, they
lose their faith because they've
stopped adoring me.

In Sinu Jesu

Dear Lord, please pass the grace I need so that all my ideas, intentions, actions, and operations may be directed purely to the service and praise of your Divine Majesty.

Saint Ignatius Loyola

What have I done for Christ?
What am I doing for Christ?
What will I do for Christ?

Saint Ignatius Loyola

I pray, joyously and generously, for a deeper awareness of the power and presence of the Spirit of Jesus at every moment.

Saint Ignatius Loyola

If you abide in Me, and my words abide in you, ask for whatever you wish, & it will be done for you.

John 15:7

O Jesus, I put my trust in Thy merciful
goodness.

In Sinu Jesu

If in my name you ask me for anything,
I will do it.

John 14:14

You must love the Lord your God with all your heart, with all your soul, & with all your strength. This is the first, and greatest commandment. The second resembles it: you must love your neighbor as your self. On these two commandments hang the whole Law, and the Prophets also.

Matthew 22:37-40

There's never time to do everything,
but there's always time to do
something.

Peter N Roth

Jesus wants **me** as a *partner*!

Peter N Roth

Group or Die.

Romans 8:6 (paraphrased)

Examine yourself to make sure you are in the faith; test yourself. Do you acknowledge that Jesus Christ is really in you? If not, you have failed the test.

2 Corinthians 13:5-6

Saint Mechtilde asked Jesus if she did not lose much in hearing the Mass from so great a distance. Our Lord said to her: "It is good to be present, but, when impossible, and when illness, or obedience, or any other legitimate reason prevents, then, where thou art, I am present."

I love you God, almighty Father
Creator of Heaven and Earth
And I love you Jesus, the only Son
Who was conceived by the Holy Spirit
Born of the virgin Mary
Suffered under Pontius Pilate
Crucified, died, and buried.
You descended into hell.
On the third day you rose again from the
dead.
You ascended into heaven to sit at the
right hand of the Father.
You will come again in glory to judge the
living and the dead.
I love You Holy Spirit, Lord and giver of
life, Who proceeds from the Father and
the Son.
With the Father and the Son
You are worshipped and glorified.
You have spoken through the prophets.
Thanks for the holy Catholic church
The communion of saints
The forgiveness of sins
The resurrection of the body
And life everlasting. Amen.

The creed as prayer

Pray without ceasing.

1 Thessalonians 5:17